LET'S LETTERB

A BEGINNER'S GUIDE

by
Janet Palmer

Acknowledgements:

My thanks to Godfrey and Anne Swinscow and Tony Moore (100 Club); John Whiting and Mike Carter (Dartmoor Rescue Group); and to the Dartmoor National Park Authority for all the help and friendly advice I have received in preparation of this booklet.

To all those members of the Dartmoor Letterbox '100 Club' whose endeavours have provided everyone with many hours of enjoyment over the years

First published in Great Britain in 1998

Copyright © Janet Palmer 1998

Orchard Publications
2 Orchard Close, Chudleigh, Newton Abbot, Devon TQ13 0LR
Telephone: (01626) 852714

Printed by
Hedgerow Print
The Old Creamery, Lapford, Crediton, Devon EX17 6AE

CONTENTS

Introduction

In years gone by friends used to ask us why we returned so frequently to an area of bleak moorland, known principally for its Prison, dangerous bogs and all-enveloping mists. Our main holiday was spent abroad but for a week in Spring and Autumn we always returned to Dartmoor.

'The West Country is such a beautiful area', they would say. 'Why only go to Dartmoor?'

I think they thought we would 'grow out of it', especially after the birth of our daughter, but it was then that we began to collect letterboxes, hoping that on our now shorter walks, she would enjoy a 'treasure hunt' and eventually develop an interest in Dartmoor itself. Our friends decided we were completely mad - after all, what sane person would roam about amongst bogs and rocks looking for rubber stamps in boxes!

We replied that, looking at it objectively, we were equally as sane as those who spent all their spare time (and a great deal of money) hitting little balls into slightly bigger holes, or those for whom an important part of summer was knocking two small pieces of wood from three stumps with a ball. We could see they were not convinced, but as time passed and we developed no other symptoms of insanity, they lowered their eyebrows and sometimes took an interest.

We now live close to the Moor and visiting friends often ask if they can try letterboxing for themselves. Our letterbox catalogue is computerised and it is a simple matter to print out the clues for an easily accessible grid square, lend them a compass and a map and send them off on a day's treasure hunt. Their walk is always enjoyable, their hunt successful in varying degrees, but their questions are numerous. 'What on earth is clitter?' 'What does a bound stone look like?' 'What does N.H.T.V. stand for?' and 'What's a logan for heaven's sake?'

This little book is for everyone, visitor or local resident, who perhaps know little about the Moor, but are intrigued by its wild, dramatic scenery and would like to try for themselves the unique treasure hunt pursued by thousands in its wide open spaces. Its aim is to make your introduction to letterboxing more successful, safe and enjoyable and to emphasise the damage that indiscriminate and careless searching can do to Dartmoor.

But be warned! Collecting anything is addictive and letterboxing is no exception to the rule!

Janet and Ossie Palmer
The Scribe and the Snapper

WHAT IS A
DARTMOOR LETTERBOX?

It all began in 1864 when James Perrot, a Dartmoor Guide, placed a sweet jar in a peat bank at Cranmere Pool as a receptacle for the cards of the people he escorted there. Cranmere Pool is in the centre of the  North Moor and a visit there in those days, involved a long walk over very rough terrain, quite an accomplishment. Now a military road runs within a mile and access is easier. The sweet jar was eventually replaced by a tin box and a book added to record the visit. Later still a rubber stamp and inkpad were placed in the box and the walker stamped a postcard, addressed it to himself and left it in the box for the next caller to take and post from a conventional letterbox. Now a granite box stands there, one of only two permanent sites, the other being at Ducks Pool on the South Moor.

By 1976 fifteen other boxes had been placed which were illustrated on a chart in order to provide interesting walks, the collection of the stamps being a permanent reminder of these excursions. The popularity of this 'hobby' grew and many more boxes were carefully hidden beneath rocks and in natural crevices all over the Moor. The stamps depicted all the varied aspects of the Moor, its legends, flora and fauna, stone circles and rows, wayside crosses and its industry, ancient and modern. Walkers carried an inkpad and a book or postcards to take an impression of the stamp and a pen to record their visit in the visitors' book.

In 1979, when the number of boxes had reached 100, a group of walkers and letterboxers met at The Forest Inn, Hexworthy and the Dartmoor Letterboxes 100 Club was formed under the leadership of retired head brewer, Godfrey Swinscow, membership being given to all who could prove they had visited 100 boxes.

The 100 Club today

The number of boxes sited on the Moor has increased dramatically over the ensuing years and although boxes can remain on site for several years, many stay for just a few months. Wherever possible, the bearings and clues for new boxes are checked to ensure they are correct, a task undertaken by volunteers.

Godfrey Swinscow still walks the Moor he loves although these days his journeys are much shorter. He began letterboxing in 1935 and his study is home to a vast letterbox 'library' which includes many beautiful drawings from which some of the stamps were made. He can no longer join the merry band of people who, on New Year's Day (whatever the weather!), tramp to Fur Tor, in the heart of the Northern Moor. In recent years he and his many friends have celebrated the occasion at the tiny Fur Tor which stands above the Yes Tor Brook, near Princetown. A popular and much loved figure, Godfrey still plays an active part in the 100 Club, taking care of all new members and joining in the organisation of social occasions such as the bi-annual Letterbox Meet.

Today 100 Club members total well over 12,000 worldwide with enthusiasts travelling many miles to pursue their hobby. There are already several Americans amongst them and in April 1998 an article on Dartmoor Letterboxes appeared in an American magazine called the Smithsonian, prompting a visit by another group of Americans wanting to try for themselves this piece of British eccentricity.

Unusually, especially in view of the efforts put in by many volunteers, no fee is charged to belong to this Club. All that is required for membership is a list of the 100 boxes collected and the approximate dates on which you found them and this should be sent to:

Godfrey Swinscow
Cross Farm, Diptford, Totnes, Devon TQ9 7NU

He will also be able to supply you with a current price list for the various rucksack badges available to 100 Club members. As well as the 100 Club badge itself, there are blue badges for 200 boxes collected, gold for 500 and for those who have visited 1,000, 2,000, 3,000 and 4,000 different boxes there are special laurel wreath cloth badges. A 5,000 badge is also available.

For many years now a team of hard-working Club members has produced a catalogue of clues twice yearly and these days a fortnightly information sheet or 'update' is available too, in order to notify members of boxes removed and put out since the Catalogue was published. The clues listed are for those boxes which have been registered with the 100 Club. Each box is registered for a period of five years and, after that time, must be re-registered in order for it to continue appearing in the catalogue. This is done to assist the 100 Club and the National Park to assess how many boxes are on the Moor at a given time but, as you will find in your travels, there are many unregistered boxes on the Moor and this makes the task extremely difficult.

Dartmoor's vulnerability to the wear and tear caused by the many people who pursue this popular hobby is recognised by all. Working closely with the National Park the 100 Club has devised a Code of Conduct for box owners and collectors which is given in detail in the chapter entitled *Looking after Dartmoor*.

Dartmoor Letterbox 100 Club Meet

This is a twice-yearly event which takes place on the Sunday of the weekend the clocks change in March and October. The venue is the Dartmoor Prison

Officers' Club in Princetown. Publication of the new Catalogue coincides with the Meet and you will be able to buy a copy here. Charity Walks are also on sale and copies of the stamps you will find on these walks are usually displayed. You will be able to see a computerised system of the letterbox catalogue which is easy to install and operate and its many features are a real advantage to those, such as ourselves, who have little enough time to pursue our hobby.

The Meet is very much a social occasion attended by letterboxers from all over the country. Many special 'one-day' stamps are available for you to collect and, of course, many of those present will be carrying their 'Travellers' as well, although sometimes these are only given as a 'swop'.

Letterboxing necessities such as white cards, stamps and stamp pads can all be purchased here, as well as a range of outdoor equipment and clothing. Books about Dartmoor and the Dartmoor Magazine are also on sale.

LET'S GET READY!

You will need:
* a Letterbox Catalogue or Charity Walk
* a map
* a compass
* a book or white cards to collect the stamp impressions
* a pen to record your visit in the book
* a rucksack to carry them in
* waterproof clothing
* something to eat and drink.

The Letterbox Catalogue

Friends who are already letterboxers could obviously be a great help in getting you started, but the Catalogue of Dartmoor Letterboxes produced by the Dartmoor Letterbox 100 Club will be an essential part of your letterboxing equipment.

The clues are listed alphabetically by the title of the box. Where a grid reference for the box has been given this follows the title. Many do not have grid references and it is left to you to discover their position on the Moor - a skill which, I assure you, will come with practice, a careful study of your map and the knowledge you will gain from your walks on the Moor. Your mental skills also will be put to good exercise as you attempt to plot the whereabouts of the many cryptic clues included!

The number following the grid reference is the registered number of the letterbox and after this comes the clue itself, most of which contain compass bearings on named features taken from the site of the box.

Towards the back of the Catalogue you will find a Walk Planner which will prove very useful. Here each grid square is listed in numerical order, with the titles of the letterboxes it is known to contain printed alongside. All you need to do is to decide where you would like to walk, check on your map which grid squares you will be passing through and list the boxes to be found there. If you want to be really well prepared you could determine from the clues the exact position of the box in the grid square and plan your route from one box to another.

How can I obtain a Catalogue?

If you are unable to get to the Meet, the latest letterbox Catalogue and the current price plus postage and packing can be obtained from:

Tony Moore
25 Sanderspool Cross, South Brent, Devon TQ10 9LR

As a rough guide, the price at the time of going to press is £5.45 plus 75p postage and packing, but this is obviously subject to change and it would be advisable to check with Tony before sending off your cheque or postal orders.

The fortnightly updates to the Catalogue are also available from Tony. The price of each update is 20p and all requests must be accompanied by a stamped, addressed envelope. To minimise the work involved should you decide you would like the updates on a regular basis, it is easier to send to him, say 10 stamped addressed envelopes, accompanied by your cheque/postal order for 10 x 20p for the updates so that he can send you a copy fortnightly as they are produced. Once again, prices may be subject to change so check the front of your up-to-date Catalogue for any increase in the cost of the updates.

Charity Walks

Curlew

I am including these at this point because, as many of them are planned with families in mind, they follow relatively easy routes and are therefore ideal for beginners. All commence at one of the moorland car parks and follow a circular route covering roughly between four and seven miles. The clues, for between 10 and 15 boxes per walk, carry bearings on named landmarks which you can identify from your map and sometimes even give directions which lead you from one box to another. The stamps provided for these Walks are always high quality and usually depict some aspect of the Moor. As you follow the route you may come across other boxes to add to your collection and such a walk will familiarise you safely with one small corner of the Moor.

Charity Walks cost in the region of £2 to £2.50, providing you with an enjoyable letterbox walk and the nominated Charity with much-needed funds. These walks usually remain on the Moor for six months, roughly coinciding with the Letterbox Meets.

How can I obtain one of these special Walks?

They can be purchased at the Meet from the organisers, but if you are unable to get to a Meet then details of each Walk organiser and where to send your cheque to purchase the clues are given in the updates, especially the three updates following a Meet. Even if you do not receive the updates from Tony on a regular basis, by sending the relevant cheque/postal order for three updates and three stamped addressed envelopes to him, specifying that you require updates 1, 2 and 3 for details of the Charity Walks, he will send these to you as they become available.

Choosing a map

We recommend a good large scale map such as the Ordnance Survey Outdoor Leisure 28 Dartmoor — 2½ inches to 1 mile. It names all the major tors, rivers and streams and clearly marks private land to which the public have been granted access. It is possible to buy these already weatherproofed and there is also a good selection of waterproof map cases on the market.

If you are unfamiliar with map reading take some time to study the map and get to know the many symbols displayed, all of which are easily identified by the key. Even on a short walk check your intended route on the map to determine the type of ground you will be walking over and whether there are any boggy areas to avoid, streams to cross or hills to climb.

What are grid references?

Grid lines are a normal feature of any map and a grid reference is used to identify a certain area. The lines running up and down the map with numbers increasing as they run East are called 'Eastings'. The lines across the map increasing as they go North are called 'Northings'. Letterbox grid references will contain 4, 6 or even 8 numbers. The four figure numbers identify the grid square only. The first two will be the number of the Easting line on the map and the second two the number of the Northing line. From my school days I remember an easy way to identify in which order they go as being 'Along the corridor and up the stairs'.

For a six figure grid reference the square is divided into segments, 10 up and 10 across the square, as shown in the diagram. This will locate an area of 100 metres by 100 metres in which the box should be. Try plotting onto your map the six figure reference of 578 742 given in the diagram. After plotting the final digit (2), (distance B on the sketch), your pointer should be close to North Hessary Tor. This diagram and a more detailed explanation also appears in your Letterbox Catalogue. If you're still a little hazy, keep practising, it will soon become much easier.

GRID REF.
OF 578 742

Choosing a compass

A simple navigation compass, such as the one illustrated, will cost in the region of £10 and includes all the features you will require, not only to determine the whereabouts of a letterbox from the bearings given in the clues, but to navigate yourself around the Moor. Compasses vary in price depending on their features and it is worth paying a visit to an outdoor centre to check the ranges available. Sighting compasses have a facility whereby at a certain setting, all you need to do is to point it at, say, one of the tors and it will give you a bearing on that tor from the point where you are standing. This type of compass cannot

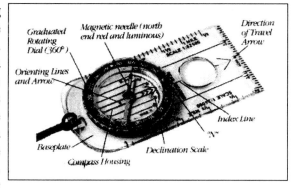

always be used for navigation in conjunction with your map, although the more expensive one made by Silva, does have this facility. Incidentally, Silva have produced a very handy leaflet called *Read this, or get lost*, so don't forget to ask for a copy if you choose one of the compasses in their comprehensive range.

How do I find a letterbox using my compass?

Many clues contain bearings on at least two named landmarks. For example: You are somewhere in the grid square 5373. The clue reads: 'Vixen Tor 057°. Tree on Feather Tor 312°.' (This is not an actual clue!). With the aid of your map identify which tor is Vixen making sure you can see it from where you are standing. Point the Index Line of the compass at Vixen Tor and rotate the compass dial until the red needle aligns with the 'N' for North. Keeping the compass steady, read the bearing given at the Index Line. From this reading you will be able to determine where you should be for the bearing on Vixen Tor to read '057°'. Repeat this procedure with the bearing for the tree on Feather Tor and walk to a point where the bearings for both these features are identical to those shown in the clue. Check your bearings as you go and adjust your direction accordingly. When your bearings 'marry up' begin a careful search for the box, taking into account any other information given in the clue.

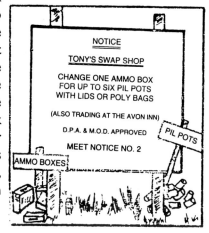

What do Letterboxes look like?

Once upon a time many were set up in old ammunition boxes, but these are not now permitted. They are bulky and not always weatherproof, requiring polythene bags to wrap the visitors' book in and to keep the stamp dry. Ice-cream boxes and similar containers were and still are used sometimes, but today's favourite containers are pill boxes which come in various sizes and many are large enough to hold a good-sized stamp. Round in shape and smaller in size than ammunition boxes or plastic cartons, they make less of a visual impact on the Moor and are also harder to find!

Each letterbox should contain a stamp and a visitors' book, although where a series of boxes has been placed on the Moor the visitors' book is usually carried in the first or last box of the series. Clues to other boxes sometimes appear in the back of the book and all visitors' books should contain the name address and telephone number of the box owner so that they can be contacted by anyone who finds a box in a poor state of repair.

Stamping up

Plain white cards or an exercise book with a stiff cover seem to be preferred by most people for recording their stamps and are easily available from stationers. If you choose to use cards avoid shiny ones as they don't absorb the ink very well and can produce 'smudgy' impressions.

You will also require an ink pad to take your impression and a pen to record your name and the date in the visitors' book. Many regular letterboxers have devised special names for themselves, such as 'The Clay Plodders', 'Far Tor', 'Bogtrotters' and 'Wobbly Bootie'. Instead of a signature they use a personal stamp to record their visit and a great deal of friendly rivalry surrounds the race to be first in the visitors' book when a new box is placed on the Moor.

Rocks are notoriously 'knobbly' and a small block of chipboard provides a firm, flat surface for taking clear stamp impressions. At the Meet it is possible to buy special wooden boxes with two compartments, the top one being for blank cards while the bottom one, accessed by a slot, will keep the stamps you have collected flat and dry.

Problems finding a box

- Make sure you are holding the compass level and steady when taking bearings and keep checking.

- Have you identified the correct landmark for the bearing? (Lone trees can be very confusing !)
- Check that your compass is not close to a metal object which may be causing an erroneous reading.
- It is possible that the bearings given are not quite correct, although most boxes are checked to ensure accuracy. Widen your circle of search a little and be thorough — some boxes are very well hidden!
- It may be that the box you're hunting for has been taken in for some reason and has not yet been reported in the updates.

When necessary put a limit on the amount of time you spend searching for a box. Too much of a challenge can prove very frustrating and, after all, you are supposed to be enjoying yourselves! However determined you are to find a box, please remember that careless searching damages the Moor and that each box should be inconspicuous when you return it to its hiding place.

Will I find letterboxes without having the clues?
Quite a few tors are accessible from the main car parks and as letterboxes are often sited amongst their rock-strewn slopes, it is occasionally possible to come across one or two on a short walk. A carefully placed stone beneath a rock or a slightly trodden-down area may indicate a box site and is worth exploring, but it may be an old hiding place or one where the box has been re-sited to prevent further erosion of the ground. As most boxes are well hidden, random searches sometimes prove very frustrating and a fruitless search can spoil an otherwise lovely day on the Moor.

Are there letterboxes in other parts of the country?
Yes there are, but not very many. I have been told there are a few on Bodmin Moor in Cornwall, on the Brecon Beacons in Wales, a few in the Lake District and on the Yorkshire Moors. The New Forest has around 900 boxes although the clues run from one box to another and are hard to come by unless you go with a letterboxer 'in the know'. I believe the New Forest boxes are growing in number and it may be that in time someone will organise the distribution of clues but, at the moment, Dartmoor remains the prime location.

Is there a letterboxing computer programme?
There are two or three to my knowledge, mainly DOS based. I believe the only one based on Windows (3.1 or '95) is the one that we have. It is a comprehensive, easy to run programme, containing all the clues in the Letterbox Catalogue with many other features. It will give you a 'report' of all the letterboxes in a given grid square(s) and print it out with the clues. There is a 'Find Where'

feature which will give an eight figure grid reference on two named bearings, a route planner and a list of places on the Moor. It is possible to purchase a monthly disc, based on Tony Moore's updates, to update the system. The price of the system itself is £25 (for those who feel like copying it all from the Catalogue!) or £50 with all the letterboxes, clues etc., and this includes the price of the first update. Updates are priced at £1 per month thereafter.

For further details apply to:
Mike Holliday
20 Forbes Close, Heathfield, Newton Abbot, Devon TQ12 6SD
☎ (01626) 835214

Young letterboxers recording a 'find'.

BUT IT'S RAINING!

There is nothing more frustrating than making all the preparations for a day out and then being thwarted by the vagaries of the weather. Dartmoor has a micro-climate all its own sometimes, with rain and cloud clinging to the Moor and bright sunshine (but no letterboxes) just a few miles away.

Never mind — most public houses around the Moor have at least one letterbox stamp behind the bar and will welcome your custom although it may be advisable to stick to soft drinks if you intend to cover a number of them in a day!

As an alternative, why not visit the Museum of Dartmoor Life at Okehampton. It contains many interesting and informative displays covering life on Dartmoor over the centuries. The entry fee is reasonable and they have a letterbox. Finch Foundry a few miles away at Sticklepath is also well worth a visit, with yet another stamp to add to your collection.

Princetown in the centre of the Moor is an excellent hunting ground. Here letterboxes can be found in all three pubs as well as in the Duchy House Tearooms, Fox Tor Cafe, The Old Police Station Cafe, and Mr Fixit (the garage). Opposite the Prison itself, and in course of expansion, is a unique Museum where many interesting items collected from the Prison over the years are displayed. Once again there is a small entrance fee and several letterboxes can be found here too.

Several of the ice-cream vans located in the popular car parks around the Moor also carry letterboxes. A firm favourite with visitors and local people alike is the refreshment van below Great Hound Tor where Alan, Hound of the Basket Meals, serves snacks from delicious burgers to home-made fruit cake and, of course, he has a letterbox.

If you feel like an enjoyable evening with fellow letterboxers, at the time of going to press, The Plymouth Get-Together meets at the Woodland Fort Community Centre, Crownhill, Plymouth on the third Wednesday evening of each month. Everyone is welcome and there is sometimes a talk on letterboxing, Dartmoor or a related topic.

The Dolphin hotel in Bovey Tracey is the venue each Wednesday evening for other keen letterboxers.

Dartmeet Clapper Bridge — Collectors Item 1902.

Dartmeet in Summer

Wintertime at Dartmeet

Dartmoor Letterbox Series — Bridge Scheduled No. Ten

PICTURES IN INK

Of the many subjects covered by letterbox stamps, some of the most beautiful pictures are of the different aspects of Dartmoor itself. Birds, tors, flowers, antiquities and industries such as tin mining and quarrying have all been commemorated by these pictures in ink. Many stamps are made from original drawings, such as the ones drawn by Eric Spicer depicting Dartmoor Bridges which Godfrey has in his remarkable collection. Tim Sandles is another artist who has designed many stamps for letterboxes. Intricate and beautiful they are a work of art in themselves. Others consist of simple text such as the series dedicated to William Crossing's book *Guide to Dartmoor*. If you ever manage to collect all this particular series you will have traversed the entire Moor one way and another! Not to be forgotten are the hours it must take some box owners to hand-carve a design on a large rubber!

Occasions both happy and sad are often marked by a box on the Moor. One called 'The Long Stretch' marks its owners' Silver Wedding and many a dog is remembered with a stamp. In the visitors' book of 'Annie's Song', near Combestone Tor, there is a poignant poem relating the tragedy which overtook Annie, a long-haired dachshund, on the Moor and which I am sure has brought tears to the eyes of many a letterbox hunter over the years.

Letterboxing has an obvious appeal to children of all ages and quite a few stamps on the Moor have been placed especially with them in mind. There are many dog's boxes, too, where dog biscuits can be found as well as the stamp — a treat from friendly canines to other dogs who love to walk the Moor. I suspect that this delightful idea may have been started by Godfrey's wife, Anne, with 'Mouse's Box' which was once out on Hound Tor. They are certainly not forgotten by the

100 Club either and there are special collar tags available for dogs who have visited 100 boxes with their owners.

A dog is a natural companion on the Moor, providing it is well-behaved - as most letterboxing dogs are — but letterboxing cats?

We watched in amazement as a couple left their car and walked off over the hill with two obedient Siamese cats running along behind. A while later we mentioned this to friends who told us that the cats were Wallaby and Sheba and that they were regular letterboxers. In fact they are mentioned in Anne Swinscow's book *More Dartmoor Letterboxes* in which Anne also tells the story of Jason, the hen, who was a great walker and regularly went on letterboxing trips with a friend of hers.

A Dartmoor Wedding

Amongst the remnants of Huntingdon Mine near the Western Wella Brook on the South Moor lie the low walls of a small building known as Keble Martin's Chapel (GR 656 666). It was built by a group of young men who camped here during the early part of the century, one of them being the Reverend Keble Martin, a well-known botanist. A simple cross is carved here on an upright stone and a horizontal rock nearby bears the CHI RO symbol. The group held their services here and also baptised a child born to the warrener at nearby Huntingdon Warren House. In this remote place eight years ago two dedicated letterboxers were married. Known to letterboxers as 'Dartmoor Deliverer' and 'Perambulating Pysgie' they mark their anniversary each year with a new letterbox on the Moor.

ARE WE HAVING FUN, YET?

Travelling Letterboxes

Many letterboxers, such as those who live too far away to look after a box sited on the Moor, carry a 'Traveller' in their rucksack. It is just like any other letterbox really and we have spent many a convivial half-hour 'swopping' Travellers on the Moor, making new friends in the process. Fourteen years ago, when we began letterboxing, the Catalogue of Dartmoor Letterboxes was only available to 100 Club members and these 'travelling' boxes were a great help towards the

14

LETTERBOX WIDOW

magical 100 boxes required for membership. So many are carried now that they are listed in a catalogue of their own and add a great deal to the sociability of letterboxing. The great British reserve vanishes into a Dartmoor mist with the question 'Do you carry a Traveller?' and frustrations caused by a box you can't find disappear with a few more hands to help in the search.

But just a word of warning — although most letterboxers enjoy swapping Travellers and anecdotes, some prefer to go about their hobby in secret and take steps to avoid other letterboxers. This same secrecy applies to '**Word of Mouth Boxes**' where clues are given only to those people known personally by the box owners, which may be a wise move as letterboxes are vandalised sometimes and the stamps are stolen.

Where can I go to get a stamp made for me?

Any of the firms listed below will make you a stamp to your own size and design and I suggest you write or telephone for up-to-date price lists. Generally speaking the larger the stamp, the bigger the cost. The design/artwork/text must be clear and sharp — the quality of the impression made by your stamp will depend on this.

Dartmoor Letterboxer

Terry & Lorraine O'Sullivan
Loricraft/Pebbles & Co.
4 Big Lane
Lambourn
Berks RG17 SXQ
☎ plus FAX (01488) 72267
☎ (01488) 73934

Ottery Press
8 Ottery Cottages
Lamerton
Nr Tavistock, Devon PL19 8NR
☎ (01822) 616295 Fax: (01822) 616294

Ink Print
3 Station Road
Okehampton
Devon EX20 1DY

☎ (01837) 52937

G Woolf
Hobby Stamp Maker
165 Witcombe, Yate
S Gloucestershire BS37 8SH
☎ (01454) 881607

SAFETY - FIRST!

For your rucksack or pocket — A handy yellow card *Comfort and Safety on Dartmoor* can be obtained free of charge from National Park Information Centres and Tourist Offices.

For those of you who are new to Dartmoor as well as to letterboxing, or if you need to practice your skills with map and compass, I would strongly suggest short excursions initially. An enjoyable day and a great many letterboxes can be found within 1 or 2 miles of a car park.

Even on a fine summer's day, strong, waterproof shoes or boots or even comfortable wellies are essential to see you safely across the small streams and patches of mire and offer the best protection for your feet against the granite rocks which lie everywhere, sometimes cosily hidden beneath grass and moss! The slopes of many tors are littered with rock streams or 'clitter', (a word with which you will become familiar as it is often used in letterbox clues) making for real ankle-twisting country.

A word about snakes...

Although Dartmoor is home to our only poisonous snake, the adder or viper, very few people are bitten by them. They quickly disappear into the undergrowth when heavy feet approach and your boots will offer good protection too. Many walkers and letterboxers carry a stick, not only to aid walking, but to check in those dark, bracken-filled holes around the rocks which may harbour something other than a letterbox. Dogs are more vulnerable as they have no boots to protect them and very inquisitive noses. Seek medical or veterinary help for any snake bite as soon as possible.

and ...the weather!

Dartmoor weather is very unpredictable and there is very little shelter from wind or rain. Check the weather forecast before you go and pack your rucksack accordingly. A sharp shower, even on a short walk, can mean an uncomfortable, soggy journey back to the car, so if there is any chance of rain be prepared for it. Even on a warm day, it can feel really chilly on the tors if there is a stiff

ICE BOX

TRAVELLER.

16

breeze, so make sure you have something warm to put on.

If you decide to make letterboxing or walking a regular hobby, good walking boots and a fully waterproofed jacket and trousers would be an essential investment. They will also help to keep the wind out! Wind is ever-present on the Moor and, although the summer breeze on the tors is very refreshing after the climb up, at other times it adds greatly to the chill factor. Shade is also hard to find, so a sun hat and sun cream are important during the warmer months.

Remember that after heavy rain even small streams can quickly become raging torrents and stepping stones are often impassable.

Mist and low cloud can quickly envelope the tors and although this may only be a temporary hindrance to your walk, it can be disorientating and sometimes quite frightening, even to those people who are familiar with their surroundings. On occasions such as this your map and compass will help you to find your way back to the car if you know how to use them properly.

Skills with Map and Compass

It is beyond the scope of this booklet to teach you navigational skills but, whether you need to learn from scratch or simply to brush up your knowledge in this respect, there are experts on hand to help you.

The Dartmoor National Park run Ranger Navigation Walks throughout the summer months. These and other Guided Walks are listed in a free Magazine published by the National Park entitled *Dartmoor Visitor* which is available at all National Park Information Centres and Tourist Information Offices in towns around the Moor. These Navigation Walks are extremely popular and must be booked in advance through the Dartmoor National Park High Moorland Visitor Centre in Princetown (☎ 01822 890414), the only Visitor Centre to remain open all the year round. If you live locally or intend taking a winter break on the Moor, it is possible that the Winter Walks Programme may also include one or two Navigation Walks, although information concerning these is not available until later in the year. Once again, check with the High Moorland Visitor Centre in Princetown for details.

WAIT FOR ME!!

Getting help!

If you are intending to walk alone in a remote area, always tell someone where you are going and the approximate time of your return so that they can check to see if you have arrived back safely. Please don't forget to 'phone them if a change of plan delays you — the Emergency Services will not be too pleased if they find you enjoying a pub meal while they have been searching for you!

It is recommended that you carry a strong whistle in your rucksack. The recognised emergency signal is six blasts every minute. A whistle can be heard when your voice cannot.

Mobile phones can be very useful but many of the remoter parts of the Moor are out of range so these cannot be relied on to summon help.

If there are two or more in your party and one of you is injured, the

person going for help must first ensure that the casualty is as comfortable and as sheltered as possible and that he/she has written down the location details so that they can give accurate information to the Rescue Services. The number to call initially is '999' and they will contact the appropriate section of the Dartmoor Rescue Group.

The Rescue Group is made up of highly trained (and extremely fit) volunteers who give much of their spare time to provide a search and rescue service, assisted on occasions by a special Dog Unit. Recently the Okehampton Section of the Rescue Group has published an excellent book entitled *Walking in Northern Dartmoor* which is full of useful information on topics such as navigation and route finding, Dartmoor weather, safety and emergency procedures. It also contains fourteen well-constructed walks of varying lengths over the North Moor and a description of the interesting features to be found on the way. All the funds raised from this reasonably priced publication go to support the Rescue Group and provide the vital equipment needed to rescue those in trouble on the Moor.

Further information such as details of talks, Navigational Skills Days and other activities occasionally provided by the Group can be obtained from the National Park Information Centres.

You will probably never be in need of their services, but please make yourself aware of all the emergency procedures before venturing far into the Moor.

Military Ranges - The Army on the Moor

One important thing to remember is that much of Northern Dartmoor is a military training ground and on certain days you will see red flags flying from the higher tors, indicating that the ranges are in use and you should not, under any circumstances, venture beyond the line of red and white poles which surround the area The areas covered by the Firing Ranges are marked on your map and you can check with one of the National Park Information Centres to see which Ranges are in use before setting out on a walk. If you do find anything which could be military debris, do not touch it — please contact the Commandant

Dartmoor Training Areas on (01837) 52241 or the local police on (0990) 777444, giving as accurate a location as possible.

Serious stuff! But I'd hate you end up like our friend on the left!

Firing notices advising where live firing will take place in the coming week appear in local newspapers, police stations, post offices and a recorded message is available on the following numbers:

Torquay (01803) 294592   Exeter (01392) 270164
Plymouth (01752) 701924   Okehampton (01837) 52939

Taking a bearing

LOOKING AFTER DARTMOOR

Dartmoor has been designated as a National Park because of its great natural beauty, the wealth of habitats it provides for birds — many of them rare — and for its cultural heritage. Nowhere else in Britain can you find such a wealth of archaeological features which speak so eloquently of the people who lived and worked here. From hut circles and stone rows of the Bronze Age to the quarries and industries of more recent times — all are here for you to discover and enjoy as you search for and collect your letterboxes.

The care of Dartmoor is substantially in the hands of the Dartmoor National Park Authority. Their work force includes specialists such as rangers, archaeologists, craftsmen, and naturalists, all working to conserve different aspects of this endangered wilderness, often with an over-stretched budget. But the responsibility for looking after Dartmoor lies too with all those who use it and especially with letterboxers simply because of the nature of letterboxing. Continuous searching over a small area can disturb wildlife habitats and cause erosion to the surface of the Moor. Some antiquities, such as hut circles, are not always immediately recognisable to those unfamiliar with them and can easily be damaged by a careless search.

As letterboxing gained in popularity and the number of boxes sited on the Moor increased dramatically, it became necessary to devise a Code of Conduct to minimise damage to this already vulnerable moorland. Consequently the Dartmoor National Park Authority, the 100 Club and representatives of landowners and graziers worked together on special Codes of Conduct which appear in the Letterbox Catalogue and are included in a special leaflet entitled *Letterboxing with moor care and less wear*. This leaflet is available from all National Park Information Centres and, as the details it contains are vital to the well-being of Dartmoor, please read it carefully and abide by the rules.

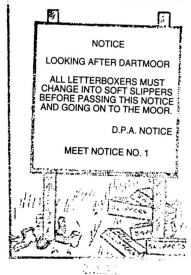

NOTICE

LOOKING AFTER DARTMOOR

ALL LETTERBOXERS MUST CHANGE INTO SOFT SLIPPERS BEFORE PASSING THIS NOTICE AND GOING ON TO THE MOOR.

D.P.A. NOTICE

MEET NOTICE NO. 1

All of Dartmoor is owned by someone, although you have a right to walk on most of it. In recent years further agreements have been made by the National Park with farmers and landowners which permit the general public to cross private land on designated footpaths. All access areas are clearly marked on your map, together with access points such as stiles where footpaths lead across farming land and through woods. It is important to remember the generosity of these landowners and to respect the privilege they have granted us.

Letterboxing Codes of Conduct

For all letterbox hunters, please ensure that:

- You search for the letterbox in a way which does not damage or disturb the land.
- You replace the box carefully and leave it as you would hope to find it.
- If you find a box in need of attention, for instance if it is saturated, you contact the owner and/or the Letterbox 100 Club who will report the fact in the fortnightly updates.

Letterboxes are not sited and you do not search for letterboxes:

- On land which does not have public access, unless the permission of the owner has been granted.
- Where they will obviously disturb wildlife e.g. on a badger sett or close to nesting birds.
- On Dartmoor's vulnerable ground - nesting bird sites from late March until mid-July, in particular the Cut Hill/Fur Tor area (GR 5982, GR 5883), Tavy Cleave (GR 5583), Headland Warren (GR 6881) and the quarries at Swell Tor (GR 5673)
- In other 'no-go' areas as defined by the National Park Authority for the benefit of conservation. These areas may be updated from time to time so please check with the Dartmoor 100 Club for clarification. Information on 'no-go' areas is available at all National Park Information Centres.
- In any kind of archaeological feature, for example in or near stone rows or circles, cists (box like structures made from granite slabs) or cairns (burial mounds), or in any kind of building (however ruined), walls or man-made structure or other artefact. If you are unsure avoid these locations.

At some point you may decide you would like to place a letterbox of your own on the Moor and this part of the Code of Conduct applies to letterbox owners:

For all letterbox owners, please ensure that:

- You look after and maintain your letterbox.
- All letter-boxes are watertight and contain a contact telephone number and/or address in the visitors' book to make sure that you can be easily

contacted if the need arises.

- Metal containers, such as ammunition boxes, are not used as letterboxes. This is at the request of the Ministry of Defence, because metal containers may become confused with potentially dangerous military debris.
- Letterboxes are placed only in existing natural holes or cavities. Under the bye-laws it is an offence to damage land.
- You try as far as possible to position your letterbox at a distance from other existing letterboxes.
- Letterboxes are not cemented in or in any other way permanently fixed in place.

To register your letterbox, the details should be sent to Tony Moore. It will be given a number and appear on the next update and in the following edition of the Catalogue.

Dartmoor National Park Visitor Information Centres

You will find a visit to one of these Centres well worthwhile. Maps, compasses and a comprehensive range of books and leaflets about Dartmoor can all be found here, plus a friendly, well-informed staff who will answer all your queries. They are situated at:

Haytor: At the lower car park on the main road. ☎ 01364 661520

Newbridge: In the riverside car park near Poundsgate on the East side of the Moor. ☎ 01364 631303

Postbridge: On the Two Bridges to Moretonhampstead Road (B3212) ☎ 01822 830272

These three Centres are open between Easter and October approximately.

The High Moorland Visitor Centre, Princetown ☎ 01822 890414 — Open all the year round. Facilities here include an interactive computerised history of the Moor, visual displays giving information on tin mining and the Moor as an Army Training ground, and an audio visual theatre. Talks on all aspects of Dartmoor are given here from time to time.

Ponies At

Crow Tor

Animals on the Moor

Many farmers have the right to graze their stock on the common land which makes up the greater part of Dartmoor.

The ponies are not really wild, they are all owned by someone and please remember that feeding them encourages them to stay close to the road and can lead to accidents.

Should you find an injured or distressed animal on the Moor there is something you can do to help. We now carry a yellow card (available at National Park Visitor Centres) giving the telephone numbers to ring for the Dartmoor Livestock Protection Society, a charity which will swiftly get help and a vet to where it is required.

Up-to-date numbers are also listed in the Letterbox Catalogue and I remembered this when we came upon a lamb trapped between rocks on Chinkwell Tor. It was weak, unable to stand and blood-stained. We found a 'phone box and telephoned the number closest to us, giving a clear description of where the lamb was to be found. We learned that evening that it had been rescued and would recover. Its injuries were superficial and it had probably been chased by a dog and fallen down the steep, rocky hillside.

It is very important to give an accurate description of the animal's whereabouts as this lamb had been reported to them on the previous day but they were unable to find it. It would not have survived another night without help.

It is also important to remember that ewes sometimes graze some distance from their offspring and if you handle an apparently abandoned lamb, the ewe may reject it.

The Country Code:

Many of you will be familiar with the general code of the countryside but any book concerning an activity in the countryside would not be complete without it

- Guard against all risk of fire
- Keep your dog on a lead or under control
- Fasten all gates
- Keep to the paths across farmland
- Avoid damaging fences, hedges and walls
- Leave no litter
- Safeguard water supplies
- Protect wildlife, wild plants and trees
- Go carefully on country roads
- Respect the life of the countryside

Fire:

In 1997 Dartmoor suffered from several devastating fires. These were not swaling fires and one at least was started deliberately, causing damage which destroyed the habitats of wildlife and rare birds. In the remote North Moor, an area difficult for fire fighters to reach, another fire raged, destroying the nesting grounds of birds and, in some places, the peat itself, which is a vital part of moorland ecology. So keep a watchful eye as you move about the Moor and report any actions or circumstances which might lead to a fire.

Litter:

I don't think we ever return from a walk on the Moor without litter in our rucksacks — not ours — other people's! It is stuffed into crevices on the tors, under rocks, in rivers and streams — just about everywhere. Few people go onto the Moor without a carrier of some kind; they brought these items with them — why can't they take them home again?

I'm not suggesting that you fill your rucksacks with rubbish, but please take your own litter home. Ring-pulls, shards of glass and small pieces of polythene can easily be swallowed by a grazing animal, causing them great suffering. Take care, too, when searching for boxes, that you don't put your hand into a crevice already occupied by broken glass!

Over the years the finger of accusation has been pointed at letterboxers in general for the increasing amount of litter on the Moor and certain acts of vandalism, often quite unfairly. In such a large group of people there will always be the odd few who act irresponsibly, giving their fellows a bad name, but the majority of letterboxers are *Dartmoor* enthusiasts too and are keen to conserve and protect the Moor — not desecrate it.

WHAT DOES IT MEAN?

Letterbox clues contain many abbreviations and items which are puzzling and very frustrating to anyone unfamiliar with Dartmoor place names and terminology. Some clues are cryptic, their solution requiring not only a knowledge of Dartmoor but the kind of brain which solves the clues in the Daily Telegraph crossword!

The Ordnance Survey Map I have suggested marks many of the tors but not all of the smaller ones. The local name for a tor may differ slightly from the one given by Ordnance Survey. For instance, Laughter Tor (GR 65 75) is a corruption of 'Loughtor' and may appear by either name in the clues. To help you I have listed below some of the most frequently asked questions and their answers.

What is meant by N.H.T.V. or TV Mast? —This is the tall mast on North Hessary Tor (GR 5774) — a landmark seen from many places around the Moor. These days it serves as a radio mast although it was once a television transmitter and several feet higher. Do not assume that 'Mast' in a letterbox clue always means this one though, there are others off the Moor which are visible and are used in some of the clues.

What does B.S. stand for? —These initials mean 'Bound Stone', a special stone, usually carrying initials, which indicates a boundary of some description. Many are easy to pick out from a distance because they are worked stones, rectangular in shape and taller than the rocks around them. Many indicate a Parish with a boundary on the Moor and are inscribed with the initials of the Parish. Some carry the initials of past landowners, or mark an area from which granite or tin was extracted. You will come across PCVWV stones (Plymouth Corporation Water Works), which mark the catchment area for Burrator Reservoir, WD stones which also carry a number from 1 to 46 and mark the old Willsworthy Firing Range, and many more. 'BS' on your Ordnance Survey map indicates a Bound Stone.

What is clitter? —This is a common name for the rock streams which litter the slopes of the tors. Caused by disintegration of the granite, it can contain enormous boulders, not always an easy hunting ground for letterboxes!

What is a logan? — A large rock which, due to the crumbling away of the granite beneath it, appears to be balancing on another. A true logan will 'log' or can be set in motion when pressure is exerted on it. Sadly, through vandalism mainly, very few real 'logging' stones remain.

What is an F.P.? — A Military Flagpole, plainly visible on days when firing is taking place because of the red flag on top of it. They stand out fairly well at other times as they are situated high on a hill or tor unless, of course, hidden by low cloud or mist.

What does RP stand for? — Range pole — red and white poles denote the perimeter of each Army Firing Range. Near Western Red Lake the three firing ranges meet, a spot celebrated by a letterbox stamp.

What is an O.P.? — An Army Observation Post sometimes camouflaged with granite and turf. There are several on each firing range and, on some of the tors on the Northern Moor, hut (huts) have also been placed for Army use, some visible from quite a distance.

How will I recognise a hut circle? — By a low, circular and usually tumbled 'wall'. They are the remains of dwellings dating back to the Bronze Age. Sometimes there are several in the same area and in some cases they are all surrounded by the remains of outer wall, as at Grimspound (GR 701 809). Occasionally the door jambs are still standing. You will not find letterboxes in the hut circles or their walls.

What is a menhir/standing stone? — A tall upright stone which sometimes stands on its own but can also be the terminal stone in a stone row. These, too, date back to the early Bronze Age. Stone rows frequently end in a circle of stones surrounding a cist or kistvaen, which once contained the remains of an important member of the community, perhaps a chieftain. You will discover many of these little rectangular stone-sided graves around the Moor, although few now have their cover stones. *You will not find letterboxes in or close to stone rows and kistvaens.*

What is a 'tare and feather' rock? — A rock split by quarrymen showing a line of rounded grooves made by the 'tare' as it was hammered into the surface.

What is a leat/dry leat? — A man-made channel dug to bring water from one of the rivers to farms, tin workings or anywhere requiring a water supply. Many are dry, but several still flow including the Devonport Leat which was dug to bring water to that town and now delivers its flow into Burrator Reservoir.

What is a bulls eye? — A stone in which a hole has been drilled, set into the bank of a leat in order to divert water into a branch channel.

What is a clapper bridge? — A simple granite slab spanning a leat or river; some consist of three or four slabs and are wide enough to carry a cart. A clam is a wooden bridge.

What is a sheep creep? — A small gap in an enclosure wall wide enough and tall enough for a sheep to pass from one pasture to another.

What is a sheep leap? — Granite blocks protruding from either side of a leat, usually placed on a wider section, to enable sheep to jump safely from one side to another.

Where and what is Brentor/Brentor Church? — This often features in letterbox clues as it forms a striking landmark situated a short distance from the Moor's Western edge. It is a sharp pointed hill, actually a volcanic plug, with a tiny Church on its summit.

What is tinners' rubble? — Many Dartmoor streams bear the evidence of tin streaming, where the early tinners extracted pure tin gravel from the bed of the stream. Heaps of unwanted rocks and stones, some now covered in vegetation, still stand beside the streams bearing witness to a bygone industry.

What does a tinners' hut look like? — Somewhere near the heaps of rock you may find the remains of a small rectangular building used by the early tinners as a shelter from the harsh Dartmoor elements.

What is an adit? — a horizontal tunnel dug into the hillside by tin workers of a later age in order to work an underground tin lode or seam. These tunnels were sometimes used to drain underground mine workings.

What is a gert? — A deep gully cut by miners to expose a tin-lode.

What is a Warren? — A rabbit farm, consisting of the warrener's house and a large area of land. Here earth and stones were piled together to form *buries* which were colonised by the rabbits. Many of these are still recognisable today and are sometimes known as *pillow mounds*.

What is a vermin trap? — These are found near the warrens and were set to trap any small animal, such as a weasel, which would prey on the rabbits. Granite slabs formed a tunnel where a trip-mechanism caused a slate to fall and trap the animal inside.

What is a peat pass? — A special track or pathway cut through an area of peat which allow easy transport for man and beast from one area of the Moor to another. Some of them were cut by Frank Phillpotts and bronze memorial plaques, known as Phillpotts' Posts, mark each end.

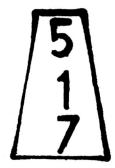

What is meant by trig or trig.pillar? — A triangular stone set on a hill or tor. These are now obsolete but were once used by Ordnance Survey to determine distances. Sometimes people 'adopt' them as an item of curiosity and these are painted white like the one on Gutter Tor.

River banks — The left and right banks of a river or stream are always determined by looking downstream with the flow of the river.

In recent years a *Gazetteer of Dartmoor Place Names* has been published, compiled by Mike Brown. This is a very useful book for letterboxers as it gives over 6,000 place names or alternative names each with an exact grid reference.

There will be other items with unfamiliar names, but those are for you to discover by a careful study of your map and by reading some of the many books written by people whose knowledge of Dartmoor far exceeds my own. If time permitted during the long winter evenings when we lived far from the Moor, a favourite occupation of mine was to sit with map and catalogue and our growing library of Dartmoor books in an attempt to find out where the ungrided and cryptic boxes were sited. I was only partially successful with the letterboxes, but the knowledge I gained and continue to gain about Dartmoor is, in itself, a source of great pleasure.

A fine example of a Dartmoor Clapper Bridge

The Author records a 'find'.

HAVE FUN!

Letterboxing is a hobby for everyone; age is no barrier; it costs very little and there are the obvious benefits provided by exercise and an unlimited supply of fresh air. Even young children can become adept with a map and compass given the right encouragement and this 'seek and find' hobby in the great outdoors can be a healthy alternative to those fascinating computer games!

The first question my grandchildren, Rebecca aged 6 and Luke aged 4, ask when they arrive is 'When can we go letterboxing, Nanna?' For them it is two or three hours of fun followed by the inevitable ice-cream, but they are already asking questions about the Moor itself and the interesting things we find on our outings.

FOUND IT

At the other end of the age scale, one of my favourite pensioners, a lady well over 70 with a replacement hip joint, still walks the Moor with her dog collecting letterboxes. She has known and loved Dartmoor since she was a child and has a wealth of tales to tell. Her dog has a 'nose' for letterboxes, especially the ones containing dog biscuits.

As with any hobby, there are letterboxers who take it very seriously indeed, planning every minute of their day and every inch of the route to collect the maximum number of boxes possible. Rain, wind or even snow prove no deterrent to these stalwarts and one clue on a recent update included a bearing on the lights in the window of a house for the benefit of night time boxers! For someone who sometimes has great difficulty in locating boxes in daylight this seems truly remarkable, but perhaps it was 'tongue-in-cheek'.

The most important product of any leisure activity is the satisfaction and enjoyment you gain from doing it. For some this may mean 30/40 boxes a day minimum; for others a good walk with lovely views and a leisurely search for boxes makes a perfect day. Whatever your preference, as you explore the tors and valleys in search of those elusive boxes and delve into books to discover place names and perhaps the answers to those cryptic clues, you may discover a new addiction, not only to collecting letterboxes, but to Dartmoor itself.

SEVENTH HEAVEN

HAPPY HUNTING!

SPRING 1997

31

BOXING CRAZY!

A compass, a map and a book full of clues
Something to eat and a strong pair of shoes.
We've been on a treasure hunt — boxes galore.
Hidden in crannies all over the Moor.
Following bearings we've hunted around
Eyes on the compass and nose to the ground.
The kids scoured the clitter and climbed up the rocks
All in the search for a magical box

We've found some hut circles, explored a stone row
(there's more to Dartmoor than boxes you know!)
We ate our packed lunch, admiring the view
Then plodded uphill for a wee box or two.
Rain drove us into a cave in the rocks
And would you believe it, there was a box!

We've squidged through a bog at a leisurely pace
Only to find we were in the wrong place!
We're covered in prickles thanks to the gorse
And our jeans smell of something that's been through a horse.
We've been quite frustrated — suffered with cramps
All in the hunt for those d----- rubber stamps!

We're tired and we're hungry but one thing's for sure
We know that tomorrow we'll go back for more!
As letterbox addicts we've all just begun
And despite a few hassles — WE'VE REALLY HAD FUN!

Janet Palmer